£4.95

EARTH HOUR

ALSO BY DAVID MALOUF

Poetry
'Interiors' in Four Poets
Bicycle and Other Poems
Neighbours in a Thicket
Poems 1975–76
Wild Lemons
First Things Last
Poems 1959–89
Typewriter Music
Revolving Days

Fiction
Johnno
An Imaginary Life
Fly Away Peter
Child's Play
Harland's Half Acre
Antipodes
The Great World
Remembering Babylon
The Conversations at Curlow Creek
Dream Stuff
Every Move You Make
Ransom

Non-fiction
12 Edmondstone St
A Spirit of Play
Made in England
On Experience
The Happy Life

Theatre
Blood Relations
Baa Baa Black Sheep
Jane Eyre

DAVID MALOUF
EARTH HOUR

UQP

First published 2014 by University of Queensland Press
PO Box 6042, St Lucia, Queensland 4067 Australia
www.uqp.com.au
uqp@uqp.uq.edu.au

© David Malouf

This book is copyright. Except for private study, research,
criticism or reviews, as permitted under the Copyright Act,
no part of this book may be reproduced, stored in a retrieval system,
or transmitted in any form or by any means without prior
written permission. Enquiries should be made to the publisher.

Cover and Design by Sandy Cull, gogoGingko
Typeset in (Garamond 11/14pt) by Post Pre-press Group, Brisbane
Printed in China by 1010 Printing International Ltd

National Library of Australia cataloguing-in-publication data is available
at http://catalogue.nla.gov.au

ISBN (pbk) 978 0 7022 5013 2
ISBN (PDF) 978 0 7022 5257 0
ISBN (ePub) 978 0 7022 5258 7
ISBN (Kindle) 978 0 7022 5259 4

University of Queensland Press uses papers that are natural, renewable
and recyclable products made from wood grown in sustainable forests.
The logging and manufacturing processes conform to the environmental
regulations of the country of origin.

CONTENTS

Aquarius   1
Radiance   2
Retrospect   4
Toccata   6
Dot Poem, the Connections   7
Footloose, a Senior Moment   8
Entreaty   10
Whistling in the Dark   12
Ladybird   14
Garden Poems   16
   Touching the Earth   16
   The Spell   17
   After   18
Inner City   20
An Aside on the Sublime   22
Sky News   24
Trees   26
Rondeau   27
Two Odes of Horace   28
   Odes I, xxvii   28
   Odes II, ii   28
Spleen   30
A Parting Word   31
The Brothers: Morphine & Death   32
Long Story Short   33
Ghost Town   34
Writers' Retreat: Maclaren Vale, 2010   35

Persimmons: Campagnatico   36
A Recollection of Starlings: Rome '84   38
Windows   40
Nightsong, Nightlong   41
Eternal Moment at Poggio Madonna   42
Towards Midnight   44
    The Cup   44
    Towards Midnight   45
    The Rapture   46
At Laterina   48
All Souls   50
Earth Hour   51
A Green Miscellany   52
    Good Friday, Flying West   52
    The Far View   53
    Haystacks   54
    Blenheim Park   55
    Cuisine   56
    At Skara Brae   57
    A Green Miscellany   58
    Sunken Garden   59
    The Bird-cages in Angel Place   60
    Dog Park   62
    The Worm's-eye View   64
Night Poem   65
Shy Gifts   66
Still Life   67

The Deluge   68
Abstract   70
Seven Faces of the Die   72
A Touch of the Sun   78
Shadow Play   79
Australia Day at Pennyroyal   80
Aquarius II   82
Toccata II   84
At Lerici   85

Acknowledgments   88

Aquarius

One of those sovereign days that might seem never
intended for the dark: the sea's breath deepens
from oyster-shell to inky, blue upon blue,
heaped water, crowded sky. This is the day,
we tell ourselves, that will not end, and stroll
enchanted through its moods as if we shared
its gift and were immortal, till something in us
snaps, a spring, a nerve. There is more to darkness
than nightfall. Caught reversed in a mirror's lens,
we're struck by the prospect of a counterworld
to so much stir, such colour; loved animal
forms, shy otherlings our bodies turn to
when we turn towards sleep; like us the backward
children of a green original anti
-Eden from which we've never been expelled.

Radiance

Not all come to it
but some do, and serenely.

No saying
what party they are of

or what totem
animal walks with them.

Tobias the street-smart
teen has his screwball dog.

For some it is stillness,
or within the orders

of humdrum
the nudge, not so gentle,

of circumstance. For some
the fall across their path

at noon of a shadow
where none should be,

for some their own
shadow seen as not.

For some a wound, some
a gift; and for some

the wound is the gift.
When they

too become one
of the Grateful Dead, it is

the silence they leave,
in a bowl, in a book,

that speaks and may join us;
its presence,

waist high at our side,
a commotion, a companionable

cloud with the shape and smell of
an unknown familiar, call it

an angel. At his nod,
the weather we move in

shifts, the wind changes.
Catching

the mutinous struck infant
in us on the off-chance

smiling.

Retrospect

A day at the end of winter. Two young men,
hooded against the silvery thin rain

that lights the forest boughs, are making towards
a town that at this distance never gets closer.

One of them, not me, as he turns, impatient
for the other to catch up, wears even now when I meet his
    face

in dreams, the look of one already gone, already gone
too far into the forest; as when, last night

in sleep, I looked behind me out of the queue for an old
    movie and you
were there, hood thrown back, your stack

of dirty-blond hair misted with sky-wrack, and when
my heart leapt to greet you, No, your glance

in the old conspiratorial way insisted,
Don't speak, don't recognise me. So I did not

turn again but followed down the track,
to where, all those years back, you turned

and waited; and we went on
together at the bare end of winter, breath from our mouths

still clouding the damp air, our footsteps loud
on the rainlit cobbled street, down into Sèvres.

Toccata

Out of such and such and so much bric-a-brac.

Cut-glass atomisers, An Evening in Paris
stain, circa '53, on taffeta.
Four napkin-rings, initialled. Playing cards, one pack
with views of Venice, the other the Greek key pattern
that unlocked the attic door our house
in strict truth did not run to. A wrist
arched above early Chopin: bridge across water
to a lawn where finch and cricket take what's given
as gospel, and even the domino I lost
in the long grass by the passion-vine
fits white to white, four voices in close canon.

Where in all this are the small, hot, free
-associating selves, a constellation
of shoes, sweat, teacups, charms, magnetic debris?

In the ghost of a fingerprint all
that touched us, all that we touched, still glowing actual.

Dot Poem, the Connections

Before I had words
at hand to call the world up
in happenings on a page, there were the dots, a buckshot scatter
of stars, black in a white sky. Behind them, teasingly hidden,
the company of creatures.

What I'd set
my heart on, spellbound, snowbound
in a wood, was a unicorn, shyly invisible but yearning, even
at the risk of being taken,
to be seen and recognised.

What I got
was the dwarfs, Grumpy and Doc;
Spitfires, tanks, a drunken jalopy. I'm still waiting, as star-dots click
and connect, to look up and find myself, with nothing I need say
or do, in its magic presence,

as from the far
far off of our separate realms, two rare
imaginary beasts approach and meet. On the breath that streams
    from
our mouths, a wordless out-of-the-body singing. On the same
note. From the same sheet.

Footloose, a Senior Moment
for Chris Wallace-Crabbe approaching eighty

An after-dinner sleep
                Not
                            a bad place to arrive at
The big enticements may be
                        a matter of memory but isn't
                  memory the dearest
                                and cheapest of luxuries
and of its kind one of our rarest
                      gifts
                              The footloose present
        Not to be going
anywhere soon
                    The being still
                              from toe
        and fingertip to wherever
at home in our own
skin
                              makes the afternoon
            as it tempers
its flame and the salt sea-air
            its touch to diminuendo

                              as the man says
            dreamlike
As of a body for the first
                time   as I recall it

                unmoored   afloat   the Bay

                              all glitters and my father
on the skyline stepping away out
of reach
                                   a new mode
                       of being O completely   Neither
               earthbound nor even maybe
sky-bound   and as I recall it
                         now
not for the first time
                   either
                              and so
               not strangely   but for the second
                                        footloose and far out in
      the foggy galaxies   in my own blue
                              dream-bubble a star as yet
      unnamed   as yet un-
                   claimed by gravity

Entreaty

After the Age of Innocence, golden brawlers
in the arms of demigods,
we arrive at the Age of Reason, credulous poor
monsters led by a dream-team
in a mad dance down loud streets into quicksand.

After that it's the Age
of the Seven Pills daily. Small mercies
restore us. Bayside air
salt-sweet in our mouths again, we set out for
the corner shop, and by some happy chance

it is still there, the same old woman keeps it.
When the doorbell shakes her
from sleep, through wisps of grey
smoke from her asthma-papers, 'What's it to be, what's your poison
this time, love?' she wheezes.

Is it a riddle? If it is
I'm lost. The ancient
grins, abides the answer. I clench my fist on the hot penny
I've brought; only now, a lifetime
later, find my tongue:

If luck is with me
today, on my long walk home, may no
black cat cross my path, no sweet-talking stranger,
no thief, no mischief-maker,
no trafficker in last words waylay me.

Whistling in the Dark

Seeking a mind in the machine, and in constellations, however
distant, a waft of breath. Re-reading space

shrapnel as chromosome bee-swarms, hauling infinity
in so that its silence, a stately contre-dance to numbers,

hums, and flashy glow-stones bare of wild-flower
or shrub, scent, bird-song, hoof-print, heartbeat,

or bones (ah, bones!) are no longer alien or lonely
out there in the airless cold as we prepare

to lie out beneath them. Even as children we know
what cold is, and aloneness, absence of touch. We seed

the night sky with stories like our own: snub-breasted
blond topless Lolitas laying out samples

of their charms beside dimpled ponds, barefoot un-bearded
striplings ready with bow and badinage, pursued

and lost and grieved over by inconsolable immortals
and set eternally adrift, a slow cascade

of luminary dust above the earth, with the companionable
creatures, bear, lion, swan, who share with us the upland

fells and meadow-flats of a rogue planet tossed
into space and by wild haphazard or amazing

grace sent spinning. Old consolations, only half
believed in, though like children we hold them dear, as if
    their names

on our tongue could bring them close and make,
like theirs, the bitter sweet-stuff of our story

to someone, somewhere out there,
remembered, and fondly, when we are gone.

Ladybird

Childhood visitors,
the surprise of
their presence a kind of grace.

Kindest of all the ladybird,
neither lady
(unless like so much else

in those days disguised
in a witch's spell) nor
bird but an amber-beadlike

jewel that pinned itself
to our breast; a reward for
some good deed we did not

know we'd done, or earnest
of a good world's good will
towards us. Ladybird, ladybird,

fly away home, we sang,
our full hearts lifted
by all that was best

in us, pity for what
like us was small (but why
was her house on fire?), and sped her

on her way with the same breath
we used to snuff out birthdays
on a cake, the break and flare

of her wings the flame that leapt
from the match, snug
in its box, snug in our fist under the house

that out of hand went sprinting
up stairwells, and stamped and roared
about us. Ladybird,

mother, quick, fly
home! The house, our hair, everything close
and dear, even the air,

is burning! In our hands
(we had no warning
of this) the world is alive and dangerous.

Garden Poems

Touching the Earth

The season when all is scrabble,
and surge and disintegration: worms
in their black café a pinchgut Versailles rabble

remaking the earth, processing tea-bags, vegetable scraps, and hot
from the press news of the underworld, the fast lane,
to slow food for the planet.

Plum-blossom, briar rose,
commingling. Overhead pure flow, a commodious blue fine-brushed
    with cirrus.
In our part of the world we call this

Spring. Elsewhere it happens other
-wise and in other words, or with no words
at all under fin-shaped palm-frond and fern in greenhouse weather.

But here we call it Spring, when a young man's fancy turns,
fitfully, lightly, to idling in the sun,
to touching in the dark. And the old man's?

To worms in their garden box; stepping aside
a moment in a poem that will remember,
fitfully, who made it and the discord

and stammer, and change of heart and catch of breath
it sprang from. A bending down
lightly to touch the earth.

The Spell

Needlepoints of light
rain pick out a web and I am caught. The garden,
its double iron-barred gate

and the prunus pushing out
on its own path under paving-stones, floats free
and trembles. It might be gravity suspended,

or an odd angle
of time that a slight glance sideways
catches so that the whole

enterprise unsteadies, no longer instant
underfoot. What centres it,
when all has been riddled through

and questioned, is the spider, dark
death's head paramour and spell
-binder. Ablaze

in solar isolation,
it dwindles at the end of its span, its spittle-thread
of inner fire unravelled

in a riot of marigolds, and the spell so light
on the senses yet so strong,
and still unbroken.

After

I bend to it willingly, this patch
of earth and its green things, in their own world
(though I hold the title to it) hungry for life

and tenure. Here they are weeds to be uprooted:
a limited easy task, the damp and crumble
I've lived with since my first

mouthful of it, the peck
of dirt I'm still working through. All round, a suntrap,
the garden-glitter of webs. Tree

-spiders that like the weeds, our late-spring sunlight
colluding, would choke
the lot to keep their hold. Live and let live? Not yet, not

here. Inside, the phone
intrudes. Another world calls and I scurry
in, struck by the coolness of a place that is all surface

polish and appliance. Too late! The message,
if there is one, hangs
in the silence, in the air

of abeyance that attends
on hasty departure: the breathless hush, lightly expectant,
of After.

Inner City

A picture-book street with pop-up gardens, asphalt
bleached to take us down a degree or two

when summer strips and swelters. All things green,
wood sorrel, dandelion, in this urban village

salad not weeds, and food for everyone, including
rats and the phantom night-thieves who with barrow

and spade tip-toe in under the windchimes to cart off virtual
orchards of kaffir limes. Good citizens all

of Chippendale and a planet sore of body
and soul that needs saving, and by more

than faith-healing or grace — good works and elbow
grease, a back set to it, compost bins,

the soy of human kindness. In the late splendour
of early daylight saving, stars regroup

for breakthrough, mynah and honey-eater tuck
their head under a wing, ants at shiftwork

in their gulag conurbations soldier on; and hunters, clean
of hand and clear of conscience, down

tools, troop home to pork-chop plastic packs, and gatherers
gather for hugs and mugs of steaming chai.

The planet, saved for another day, stokes up
its slow-burning gases and toxic dust, gold rift and scarlet

gash that take our breath away; a world at its interminable
show of holy dying. And we go with it, the old

gatherer and hunter. To its gaudy-day, though the contribution
is small, adding our handsel of warm clay.

An Aside on the Sublime

A Ground Thrush,
the latest of many such
occasional companions,

is scribbling the dusk
with its signature
tune, a high five

sol-fa-sol-fa-doh, at each
da capo plainly astonished
by its own sufficiency.

I stand and listen,
happy to yield
the day, the scene, the privilege of being

the one here who will embellish
the hour with all it needs, beyond
silence, of manifesto. Which

the land, as it breathes out warm night
odours and settles,
takes as an usher's

aside on the sublime.
A footnote, Eine Kleine Background Music,
to its blindfold, trancelike

descent into the dark
to bring back
tomorrow.

Sky News

A listening post
in an open field,
a green message tower,

each filament and pad precision
-designed to pick up
what the four

winds and their attendant
weathers pour in,
on the senses, on the skin.

We catch
at a remove what passes
between packed leaves and Heaven's

breath as the big sky
story blows through
the gaps in conversations,

caught without
shelter like Poor Tom
under the wet lick and whiplash

of the metaphysical dark.
Hunkered down
in the raw, a-shiver between

on the one side a mad
king who weeps and blusters,
on the other his Fool

who wisecracks and mocks,
he grits his teeth,
hugs himself

to keep warm, and privy to all,
illustrious nosebleeds, the heigh-ho
Dobbin and full cry

of the great world's
hiccups and fuck-ups, says
nowt, sits out the storm.

Trees

Trees have their own lives, simple
if seasonally haunted;
in their branches the sky
-adventures of passing gods.

They make up the wood
we cannot see, and one
looks so much like the next that we
wonder what sense they have

of being what we would be
when nomad thoughts possess us, standing
in one place only with nowhere to go
but upwards or deeper.

They wear our rough hearts linked;
mute journals of what we felt,
avowals made
before rock and cloud as witness, X loves Y

forever. A promise kept
here and here only,
in their lives not ours, though the wound
still aches, in all weathers.

Rondeau

As long as
the stock keeps turning
over   as long
as spring keeps knocking
on wood and willows bud

as long as
Jane and Jed and Lou are still rocking
on and have got
my number   as long as
a wet weekend in bed

with you in chill November
just the two
of us and maybe Sting
as long
as long as a piece of string

Two Odes of Horace

Odes I, xxvii

I'm over it, the floral
tributes, fancy speeches.
Thank you but

the roses in that bouquet, so pretty
pink, will be ash-grey
by nightfall.

From now on
I'll take life straight, no fuss,
no faddle. So fill

the wine-cup, boy, and stand
close by in the vine-leaves' fretwork
sunset while I drink.

Odes II, ii

It's the coin in use, the blade
in action that means business.
Stacked in a vault, locked up
    in rifts in the Sierra,
        all minerals are dross.

It's the world's big-time big spenders
who hog the news. Big bucks
stop nowhere. Endow a college, cast
    a pearl, say La Peregrina,
      to a call-girl or an ex.

Fortunes are hard to manage.
Far easier to rule
the Russias, take a bowl
    of tea with a fat-cat Chairman,
      bring Cuba to heel.

Greed is like dropsy;
the body bloats
then parches, feeds on itself,
    hoards its toxic
      water in hundredweights.

Is Nixon back? Do millions
flatter him and chatter
of History's favourite son?
    Well we dissent, and wish
      that wise men would use better

terms. True honours rest,
the laurel, the diadem,
on the head that is not turned
    by the flash-bulbs' pop when Jackie
      O descends on the room.

Spleen

I'm like the king of a rain-soaked Low Country, young,
rich, effete, grown old before his time,
and bored, bored to extinction by his kennel
of fawning grey preceptors, his dogs, his roe-deer,
his falcon, all his beasts, and the people howling
for bread at his forecourt gate. Even Sir Fool,
his shadow once and bawdy dwarf familiar,
now stales, a peevish sad-sack. The great bed
where he's laid, with its fleur-de-lys, has become his tomb,
and the ladies who surround it, for whom a prince
is Bold always, or Fair, as they toy with a tie-string
here, an eyelet there, raise in this death's head
no spark of the old quick leap to concupiscence,
nor can alchemists, as they fossick and assay
his stools, sniff out the prime cause of corruption
in him, or bloodbaths, in the high Roman style
passed down by senile tyrants, revive in organ
and nerve dulled to stupor a warmth past all
rekindling, manly vigours now long spent.
Not blood swells these writhen veins but the green putrescent
slime that clogs the slow tide of Lethe.

After Charles Baudelaire, 'Spleen'

A Parting Word

All's dashed in me, all's dished and done,
bold schemes, fond hopes, my long dispute
with a sick world, one man's concern
for his own and others' troubles. Death
is the next big thing. It's all I've got
to live for now. To live with.

E finita la commedia, last lines,
then curtains! The public, my loyal fans,
with a yawn troop home to supper. A chorus
or two, a pint or two — 'The ladies,
bless 'em!' — a few good laughs. It's not
so dumb to love life. He got it pat,
that hero that Homer praised. 'The puniest
live petit-bourgeois dormouse
in Dudsville SA is in better shape
than I am, Great Achilles. First
in rank of the resident zombies. Top
dog in this dog-house, Hades.'

> After Heinrich Heine, 'Der Scheidende'

The Brothers: Morphine & Death

The likeness so close between them: both
youthful, both manly fair; only one
is paler — more strict I'd say, more aloof,
more lordly. When the first drew near, how sweet
his smile, his gaze how gentle. The wreath
he wore when his brow touched mine gave off
a musky odour — poppies, but not
for long, alas, drove out the pain
I'm racked with. To be well again, quite well,
the other more stern unsmiling twin
must come and with lowered torch light up
the path that leads underground. To sleep
is good. Death's better. Best of all
were never to have been born.

    After Heinrich Heine, 'Morphine'

Long Story Short

The Book of Grievances has its roots
in singular griefs. A man keeps his list,
his hit list. Writes down times
and places where the knife went in, was twisted. Writes
it down in the ample folder of
his heart as we call it, to be underlined
in red and revisited. The gun he keeps
oiled is also there in the heart's darkness.

He takes it up and aims. Somebody falls, only he knows who
and where. In the place where grief
began and the wrong was done. When the dead
are as many as his griefs and the books are balanced he too
will be done.

        The book, like the gun, is as warmly secret
in him as hoarded sweets. Along with the rough plan
    sometime soon
to light out to the Territory, and once
gone send back no message.

Ghost Town

A bunch of five
tombstones. Toppled clouds, pillars of salt.

No footsteps lead
away. Only passers-by on the highway.

A habitation
made to be abandoned,

like a wardrobe, lopsided
on open ground and empty.

Pegged to the breeze a tee-shirt
swells with body heat.

The intruder
goes ghostly, steps through himself

and the midday glare off mica
to instant eternity.

Writers' Retreat: Maclaren Vale, 2010
for Rose Wight

I
The lake too has retreated, but the waterbirds plane in
and settle for what's there. A sky's glass ceiling
to break through. Liquid enough to make a splash.

II
Grey geese in a Quaker squad, having no word
of French, having never heard in their plump assurance of foie
gras, look neither left nor right as they wheel en masse across the
    road.

III
At dusk the cockatoos. Sulphur-crested riotous punk angels,
dropped from a clear blue sky and screaming blue
murder as they havoc the eucalypts.

IV
Under wings of sunlit spray from twitchy sprinklers
a currawong struts the lawn. All mine. All this is
mine. I'm the kingpin here. The cock, the peacock.

Persimmons: Campagnatico

Approaching February
like any other
armed camp, with
caution, one eye open
in the dark. Boughs vacant,
black, budded with ice.

Tufa-block walls
glisten with the track
of creatures of no substance.
Sluggish, damp
invisible sky-wrack.
We dig in,

prepared should things go bad
to dig ourselves out,
and might, given
the glare off so much whiteness,
go spare, save for the saving
grace, on bare

branches down there
in the mist, of luscious
red-orange, ripe-in-their-thin-skin
persimmons, pulpy
-transparent with frost.
Improbably festive

balloons — some
thirty, no thirty-one
winter suns. The air
throbs, glows bronze and sensual.
We count them, the days
of March. Considering April.

A Recollection of Starlings: Rome '84

A flight
   of starlings at dusk
                       the wing-clatter
   of a typewriter
            scatter
     of letters as a poem
gathers and takes shape
                  Once on the page
   and stays   keeps its form   Once as a storm-cloud
   shadow
       swoop
of one wing of the Avenging
   Angel above
               bridges across sky
-lit water

   An airborne crowd
                 that balloons
and buckles
        stoops to a sea-wave
   scoop
      breaks up
   in particles
        regroups
and hip-sways in tornado-twists above the Eternal

    City
           then
                    like smoke rolls off and
clears
    A new draft
  of sky
         A clean sheet
of daylight

Windows

The carpenter has arrived bringing windows.
He unpacks them from the dark
of a van, carries them in,
stacks them slant against a wall.

They are blank and do not brighten
with dawn. No stars
pinpoint at nightfall
their squared-off polished depths.

I go at different hours
to consult them
for the view that might show in which direction
the house looks, or what

season is coming
to us over the hills.
The darkness of the tradesman's
van refuses to lift. He has made windows

to a place I do not want
to go and will be back
on Friday to fit them.
I ordered and paid for this.

Nightsong, Nightlong

Below in a garden
thicket, out
of sight under moonstruck leaves, a scrap of dark
that sings. But no more dark,
because it is unseen and the night
so wide that surrounds it,
than the heart, which is just its size
in the body's dark, and hidden.

Small miracles, both. Hour
on hour without cease,
assured, lightly insistent,
they beat against stillness.
I'm here. I'm still here.
Still now and listen.

Eternal Moment at Poggio Madonna

Miss Mischa in her cool
reclusion curls on the mat.
Has a feel for
creaturely comforts and has sniffed out
this spot, though nothing
in nature or that the eye
can see marks it as special.

The sort of animal
warmth that a cat
is drawn to in a cold house; as if
the sun, centuries back,
in a burst of candescence,
had danced there, and the glow of
its presence can still be felt,

or a young god happening by had stopped
a moment to shake
a pebble from his shoe, and found
his soul struck by a mortal
dweller of the place, and the bewilderment
of instant attraction, eternal
loss, still draws him back.

Miss M. has found it out. Basks
in the sun's warmth even
at midnight; dreams of a cat
that sleeps inside the sleep
of one who, without waking,
from his tall cloud leans godlike
down and lovingly strokes her.

Towards Midnight
for Joan Tesei (1934–2005)

The Cup

In the one cup
darkness, espresso black
night, its distances,
its brief proximities,
and the arrayment
of sunlight on a sill.

I drink at the open window
heady mouthfuls
of breath, as the body,
guardian angel
of the ordinary
and of this world, reassembles

what sleep for a time
has scattered; all
the parts and occasions
of a singular story
on the instant
recalled as if new given.

An intimation of the Eternal
Return, or bitter-
sweet in the same cup, this draught
of absolute dark that shadow
-like we carry in us. Sometimes
lightly. Sometimes not.

Towards Midnight

Always at the margin
of a room, among the shreds
and shadows there, a stranger.

Upstart angel
of unease or mute disruption,
visitant lurker

with a knife for us, the killing
word we dare not speak.
Or blear-eyed, wayworn, waif-like,

the guest we have set
a place for, arriving
late for the feast.

The Rapture

The being seized
and taken.
The being
swept off your feet
by your own
breath;

the moment
and all
time no longer
on your hands.
A lightening. As if
in the nest of your palm,

an egg, its shell
as fragile and pale
blue as the sky
overhead, suddenly trembled
and cracked
open as your self

-containment might,
and you
staggered under the advent
of wings.
The loss of
gravity, the weight

-lessness of being
swept up and
taken,
less
a breaking than a breaking
out.

At Laterina
for Jeffrey Smart (1921–2013)

This waiting is no sweat. Centuries pass
unnoticed here; it's days that are tedious:
worn flagstones rubbed by skirt-hems, cart-wheels, clouds
of starlings, the boys with talent picked off
in gang-wars, gone in mobs to colour a wall
for some grim Generalissimo Lord Toad
of the Marshes, or further still to paint a prairie
hamlet in Iowa etruscan red.

The tiglio is in flower — it must be June
come round. In every street down from the station
in every village in Tuscany your journey,
this month, ends with the same sweet loaded breath,
a bee-note in the head that busies on
to a known tune, some workshop where the world
is one with our five senses. Was it always
like this? Did native sons high on a scaffold

in Piedmont, streaked with smuts in a smoky canefield
near Innisfail, North Queensland, feel the planet
shrink in their memory of it, the streets, the decades
one as each June makes them when we catch
on a gust of heated air, as at a key-change,
its green, original fragrance? — an ecstatic climbing
down and coming to earth, in their fist this dirt
a province, thick in their heads a local tongue.

Drive slowly, Jeff, take care. I'm settled, back
to a limestone wall, in the dense light of tiglio.
Whole centuries pass, the arras swings, gilt tassels
puff and trumpet dust; the oracles
of life and death, arrayed in the same shirt-sleeves,
lean down. Betrayed by audible soft collisions
of air with air, their cool mouths bring us silence.
We miss the words, old friend, but catch the sense.

All Souls

Shadow of leaves on a blind.
Ghostly, backlit,
stirred by a breath. Earth
lovers come back to bed,
to their own kind
drawn, the living, the dead
sharers of occasions.

Reclaimed the ecstatic
minute. Mouth, warm belly
within touch, reach
again. As if with a swing
summer was back, the long dark
done with, and nothing
lost or come too late.

Earth Hour

It is on our hands, it is in our mouths at every breath, how not
remember? Called back
to nights when we were wildlife, before kindling
or kine, we sit behind moonlit
glass in our McMansions, cool
millions at rehearsal
here for our rendezvous each with his own
earth hour.
            We are feral
at heart, unhouseled creatures. Mind
is the maker, mad for light, for enlightenment, this late admission
of darkness the cost, and the silence
on our tongue as we count the hour down — the coin we bring,
long hoarded just for this — the extended cry of our first coming
to this ambulant, airy
Schatzkammer and midden, our green accommodating tomb.

A Green Miscellany

Good Friday, Flying West

This knot the breeze unpicks. Our jet-stream flaps
and ripples, lays a trail
of thunder over the earth. Stars

dissolve, the pluck and flow of the planet takes us
back, half a day
or centuries; driftways

descend from Mt Ararat. Unrisen
ahead the dazzling dinning bee-hive cities.
Museums not yet open. Artefacts

in the minds of town-dwellers
waiting to take shape
at dawn: the pitcher swelling

in shadow on a shelf, the bowl
of wheatgrains on its altar still unbroken
Eocene clay, undreamed of in the earth.

The Far View

Clearly at this height the earth unravels
its secrets: cloudstuff melting, smoke
from the tripod's mouth, a fume of laurel leaves
and the long glimpses forward
to a boar's-tusk rough-rock landscape
utterly transmuted. Oakwoods

level out, the gods
go underground as hot tracks in the mind
are criss-criss-crossed with glittering plough-furrows
this morning, a doomsday map
of one-street villages
laid out under the crops,

lanes that deepen as lives go on in separation
to bone-park, cattle-market. They are there
still, unseen from highways at eye level,
a future shaped by Land Acts
not yet formulated, rippling the brow
of labourers at dawn who wade through cinquefoil stars towards it.

Cider bubbles climb
from blossom centuries off, a blade makes passage
for nuances of green. Field
after field cuts back
the dark in the mind of hungry generations. Enlightenment!
Bread in the mouth, a sharp stone in the fist.

Haystacks

The whole field stalk on stalk, scythed, gathered, stacked
in conical, low-pitched ricks, loose monuments
to use and frugal plenty. A platoon of pup-tents

on hard ground, and those whose last sleep rocked
them clean out of their skins, whom midnight drank
through straws or whistled tunes on, gone through the needle's

eye these haycocks hid. They make arrangements,
with red, with mauve, with green; approach such colour
as a spyglass finds when sun with dry thatch meddles,

or acid with blood, implausible hot pink,
the tin-sheet breath that sheds throw off combusting
at noon. Bundles of antique spills imagine

a life in the field again, pitched bale, heaped barrow.
Each straw sounds with its own voice, re-enlisting
in the loud ruck of things. Bent scarlet backs

unhump and ease off indigo. In row
on row, blond shock-heads dazzle, a world at dawn.
The one side sleet, the other sun-burst yellow.

Blenheim Park

This green park might be nature as
we dream it: a stand
of shade-trees, level grass, cattle grazing
peacefully as shadows
enter the slow mouths
of centuries this still untroubled forenoon.

In fact a battle plan
is laid out here. Thousands
of dead under the topsoil
in High Germany
stand upright still in lines as in the rising
groundfog of dawn,

the entire battle-order as it formed
in the Duke's head plainly visible
but still at this distance;
the first musket not yet smoking, the breath
of whole battalions held
in a green pause as the Commander's raised hand

freezes. No one
squeezes an index finger, no one falls. Cattle tow
their shadows through the lines, birds
dip in and out, flies tumble. The dead, dismissed
from history, go over
to nature, striding tall over the lawn.

Cuisine

What magic's here? Unique
ephemeral abracadabra
of whipped-up light-as-air
-on-the-tongue unstable Nature
reorganised, translated;
matter for mouths that is not speech.

On our lips the syllables
reshape themselves to cherry,
avocado, apple;
in the sweet flesh-fact of
a hand to mouth existence
grow round on their consonants.

A spell reversed. The garden
dissolves, goes back to breath.
Taste is the name
of things in a new language. Plain
fare, though we sit
down as to a feast.

At Skara Brae

Whistled up out of the dark,
and braw and bonny,
the old ones young
as they were again, clod
-clumsy in wellingtons,

but light as they go,
in homespun shirt and pinny,
vaulting the windrows;
at thump in the shining
gap between tomorrow

and yesterday, calling
wet seed to furrow
and blossom to bough.

The big wheel tilts, one moment
in sunshine, the next
in darkness six feet under
a field where grass-heads whisper
together under the scythe.

The chill air wraithed
with the heat of their bodies'
breath, as braw and bonny
they change, change partners,
in a slow dance with earth.

A Green Miscellany

Our Earthly Paradise: orchard blossom out of Asia
melts on the tongue as flakes of cherry strudel; the New World crams
our mouths with kartoffelsalat. No, not nature but a green

miscellany, our years-in-the-making masterpiece, as grain
on grainfield, line by line of a mute Georgics, leaf by leaf
— plane, willow, almond, palm — we labour to leave the centuries

a new and nearer version of pastoral, the diaspora
repealed in which even plants fled to the four ends of the earth,
and Eden recreated. It is making still. Even New South Wales

is one of its scattered seedbeds ploughed anew for its floreat.
Macquarie's five towns find, after twenty decades, the Home Counties
their names are homesick for. On Windsor Common, St Matthew's
    sun-parched

colonial parterre, in Richmond's water-meadows fringed
with poplars of Lombardy, the past awaits us. The law translated
more than human riffraff. Smart newly-weds who grub out all

the old-world garden shrubs and their sick fables, Olympian lust
or sin, to make a wilderness hard won from trim suburban
perches, lie down nightly in a forest, feel the ice-sheet

clink under their chin. Another garden is unlocked
in this and trusted to us. Small plots are watered in the shadow
of blackened chimney-stacks by men in shirtsleeves between shifts.

Sunken Garden

A day already
downstream of the sun
and a country of its moment
of measure. Out of slack and straggle brought
into line, into curve and square
as pleasance, and let go.

Grey slab fence-post
and rail, sagged and split. In swamp water
bristleheads of straw.

And these half-dozen
flags that raise their blue out of the mould?

Of a sunken garden
remainders. Of the blue skirts of girls
as they sweep towards occasions,
or from them, reminders.

Barefoot
on grass, children at leapfrog, or practising
the breathlessness of statues
here, when there were lawns.

The Bird-cages in Angel Place

The bird-cages in Angel Place
are empty of angels, as they are
of parakeet and songbird, their flight

into silence recorded,
Golden Warbler, Regent Honeyeater,
Superb Fairy-wren,

in grave plaques, buffed granite,
in the pavement underfoot.
Should we assume

a habitat forever
lost where once they were
our common and garden

companions, or as eternity
puzzles itself out,
a time still to come when all

the cage doors will fly open and a dazzling
emptiness break loose,
a philharmonic

consort of tumblers
in air, with viol and panpipe
and heartbeat and clamorous

wingbeat reclaiming
the currency of daylight
traffic. In blazon

and flash, the clarion
colours restored
of empery and dominion.

Dog Park

Trees of a dozen shades, all of them native,
none from the same
habitat or region, though the breezes visit them equally,
and the bees. Free access
also to civil beasts, the preened
and petted that when they heel
and prance are ghost-dancers on the feet of sleeping wolves.

The scent trail across country blurs and is lost
at a boundary fence. Communication
is minimal, the greeting
codes more intimate-curious among
the creatures, who know
no shame and are free to follow
their noses into places better not named

or noticed. We have all come a long way
to get here, the memory
of meadow-shine a green
reminder of what we were, what they
were, how we have lived and learned from
each other, and who it was that emerged
as the namers and keepers. Long-sighted stargazers, herders

of space into viable chunks, moody diviners
of closeness and the degrees
of melancholy distance, with all
that ensued as entailment:
dog-tag, poop-scoop,
dog-whistle; the angel gate
of exile. Beginning with our own.

The Worm's-eye View

Of what close up is freaked and freckled, riven
from the fresh thumbprint concordance
of what might make it perfect. The vandal's
mark. In random speck and swell a worm's-eye
deckle-edged revision. Mayhem. Maul.

From far off all
looks soulful, the monastic
hush and classic calm
of a vast library sleeping, leaf on leaf.
One style of beauty.

This other's of a more fretful sort. Unfixed from
its law, the green shoot withers. Small mouths take
in, pour out sticky web and spitball.
Unmaking, or with saw and riddle making
their own thwart commentary on the sacred text.

Night Poem

The night poem writes itself
in the long middle watch; turns up on a notepad on the night table, site
of happy collisions,

stones at a cracking pace that skip skip skip to take
the shine off glassy mornings. A shot at
the sorrowful exactitudes, where if and if only

are shifts in a plot, some of them real
disasters. The night
poem, like the night, has a habit

of slipping away, of creeping back under
a stone in the boneyard, into a mouth
whose silence is a black joke, a deadpan

tale told among drifters on the high plains of sleep.
A leaf, a leaflet blown in
at dawn out of border country.

Shy Gifts

Shy gifts that come to us from a world that may not
even know we're here. Windfalls, scantlings.

Breaking a bough like breathy flute-notes, a row
of puffed white almond-blossom, the word in hiding

among newsprint that has other news to tell.
In a packed aisle at the supermarket, I catch

the eye of a wordless one-year-old, whale-blue,
unblinking. It looks right through me, recognising

what? Wisely mistrustful but unwisely
impulsive as we are, we take these givings

as ours and meant for us — why else so leap
to receive them? — and go home lighter

of step to the table set, the bed turned down, the book
laid open under the desk-lamp, pages astream

with light like angels' wings, arched for take-off.

Still Life

'Sit like an apple', the Master grumps, and holds her
with an eye like God. She settles
in the green glade of her flesh. Gives up all thought
of her wet boots, or of hot drinks or handsprings, the animal
heat of her rain-damp skirt.
Considers herself anew as one of the crisp Calvados apples she can smell
in their dish on the dresser shelf. Lets the light-rimmed sunlit
roundness take her weight
and contain her. An isolate small
planet. Remote, green. Belonging neither
to the orchard bough it sprang from, the blossom it was,
nor to autumn or any other season. Simply
there in its ample still-life self-containment like an apple in a blue
dish on a dresser shelf in a room high up in
the twelfth arrondissement, under the eye
of the Lord God who will one day perhaps make an honest woman
of her. Not quite meaning to snatch his soul,
but making herself
in her stilled, eternal presence, real as an apple
to him, as his hand
moves through the quickened air towards our common
and garden-green beginnings. The taut round
of a belly. The swelling soft round of a thigh.

The Deluge

When roads become mirrors, who knows
where they lead? Destinations lie
on the far side of clouds and keep moving.

Turmoil: a universe
turned upside down and backwards, below
above, above and far-off under
foot. Waders, thigh-deep
in cirrus, practise a new mode of flying.
Slower. Without wings.

Begrimed, soaked, dripping,
angels take on
a second job as porters: two
with a sofa, one, arms raised, bears on his head a rare
four-legged domestic beast, a bentwood
side table; another, an old lady in a nightgown but not
perhaps in her perfect mind, who, rough-handled
with tough love, giggles to find herself
airborne and on the move — without weight and with the sky,
which is also moving, and fast,
beneath her — through a lightscape of the fallen,
or risen or still rising.
                        An antique
scene brought close. Inverted. Antipodean.
A world in panic flight

but casual. Half-comic. Out of whack.

Downhome and classic.

Unreal.

Abstract

First paint me daylight
crystals of air
out of which an iceberg
builds. Add

in touches the arctic blue
of an eye, the fixed stare
of the ice-sheet across which
five trained snow-bound explorers

stagger, then the precise
degree of nothingness
where each one comes
to a standstill and drops.

You call this abstract?
What of the hand,
its blood-warmth as it grasps
the concept 'absolute cold'?

What of the mind
that shapes what is still
air but on a snowflake's
lacy geometry raises

a cliff tall as a sky
-scraper? What of the fear
-lessness of making Nothing
so actual that white

on white as we approach it,
our hearts are stopped
mid-sentence to marble?
At a stroke, on a breath.

Seven Faces of the Die

I

That nothing is mere or only.
That not even white, seen
rightly, is without
its heat zones, gradations

of red, yellow, green,
or snow without its blue
occasions when birds fly
over, or skies change their thoughts,

to say nothing
of mind, its happy knack
of changing as it changes things
or warms to the matter.

Finding in breath
and sound-stuff much
that is more, not mere, and many,
not only. As a stretch

of fallow under ice has overtones
of clover and poppy,
and the sound for, the colour
of these, makes of the still earth's airy

stillness a slow dance; and of
its silence, as the rustling
of silk in a darkened room makes the deepest dark
chromatic, a blind man's music.

    II

Not a leaf, not a stitch
of our own. How stark we are,
how needy.

But a pencil line
on a blank page will conjure
space, volume, prospective

horizons to make for.
Kids' stuff but a beginning.

Between our fingers
and the stars all the room
in the world. And needy

is good, and bafflement.

On all fours then upright
-unsteady we set out.
What we meet

on the way, before
we get there, is the story.

And we never do
get there. Needless to say.

   III
  for Jaya Savige

At hazard, whether or not
we know it and wherever
we go. Without it no

surprise, no enchantment.
There is law enough all about us
in almanack and season, anniversary

days come round, the round earth's carnivale
of chimes and recessionals.
Good to be included

there. Good also what is not
fixed or sure even,
the second breath of being

here when the May-bush
snows in mid-September, as giddy
happenstance leads us

this way into
a lost one's arms, or that way
deeper into the maze.

    IV

This side and the other
of silence: white
noise. The snowy

infinite beyond
Happens and Becomes where nothing is

to be counted on,
and nothing
is accounted as loss.

    V

That this is our element:
a world of nine-day
wonders and other gaudies;
of road-show
rowdies in passage
from Here to Nowhere; a cortège

of all that is of flesh
and air permitted its fol-
derol and brief grandezza.
To swank, prance, cartwheel
and flare before our eyes
a moment, before it dies.

    VI
The Wager

In the air a flipped
    coin (and so many
breaths suspended on it)
    that never comes down.

    VII
for Andrea Stretton (1952–2007)

Sprigs, outbreaks of bloom, the everywhere
greenness of grass,
as the dead come to air again
under fencewire that holds nothing
in.

On slopes in sunlight
cow-parsley, lad's love,
speedwell, baby's breath, weeds
of a planet that is all
abundance and consummate
waste and replenishment.

The riot and sweet rot
of what's to come.
The life beyond corruption.

A Touch of the Sun

Earlier than the sun
and stronger, our need
for comfort in the dark.

Always on cue
with its doodle-do and smallgrass recitativo
we take the sun

as given, its shadow-play
of slats on a bed-sheet
(a hot thought

in a hot shade) semaphore
to the blood that knows nothing
of distinctions, dawn

from dusk, May from December.
Or in a deck-chair within sight of
the road,

and of rain-pool and melon-flower,
what sunlight
is to old bones.

Shadow Play

Asides of self:
verb-trash and noun-mash,
heroic strut and banter, till the eyelids

come down, not in finale
but the weariness that follows
faint applause and truce.

All actors know it, the ill
fit at knee and elbow
of another's skin. Choose silence, a sunlit

corner of afternoon,
till rabbits, tumbled from hats
that hang in the hall, resume, set on

by starshine, their antic
affray, their shadow
-play, out on the lawn.

Australia Day at Pennyroyal
for Mandy Martin and Guy Fitzhardinge

An excitement in the grass, tiny noises,
cries from underground.
Nothing on a grand scale.

But as a likeness
caught, that makes of evening as it comes on
a personal arrival,

with something to it
of theatre, something of music.

In the beholder
a willing suspension.

The day like any other
day has no memorial but itself,
and needs none. But a star, the first

and only, wades in
as expected, out of the blue. To its kin,
the small-folk of the grass a tall night-walker.

In its wake
the satiny milk-white bridal
train of infinity. Or this dazzling

hand-fling and scruple
of it, the slow shower of the galaxies.

Aquarius II

Swimming through space
this morning with the light of the Pacific
on three walls and a feathery

pink in the sky as of an angel
event. Time that can be
the devil on occasions,

in weather such as this seems bountiful, pure
gift with nothing to pay, one breath
then the next freely delivered — at least for now

and here. Elsewhere the world
kindles and quakes, women bear
on their heads a hodful of it

from one side to the other of the globe, children cram
their belly with its mud,
in a lakeside wood

anemones feel their way out of the dark
and the first four downward
notes of K.581 take a second breath and swing

companionably upward — sheer miracle
or happy accident, one, like us,
of many. With a quiet thankyou to the planet

for snow, hoop pines, Mozart,
and you of course, and you, I leave the room
to its play, sacred perhaps, with salt and sun-motes.

Content, now the little drummer has made his ado, and fax
and fiddle have had their say, to call it
a night, call it a day.

Toccata II

A man sits pen in hand, paper
before him. What is on his mind
he will set down now, the word not to be spoken

lightly. As if of all
his words this was the one that touched the heart
of things and made touch

the last sense of all as it was the first, and the word
that speaks it loaded
with all that came strongest, a planet's-worth

of sunlight, cooling green, the close comfort
of kind. It is the world he must set down
now, also lightly, each thing

changed yet as it was: in so many fumblings traced back
to the print of his fingertips still warm upon it, the warmth
that came when he was touched.

The last, as he sets it down, no more than
a breath, though much
that is still to be grasped may hang upon it.

At Lerici
for Carlo Olivieri

Darkly at anchor
in the roadstead, ships keep close
the secret of their journeys,
and the islands theirs.

History is made up
of nights such as this when little happens.

Lovers in their beds
whisper and touch, a new player
tumbles onto the scene.
Crickets strike up
a riff on the razzle-dazzle
of starlight, then stop.

The blissful friction and pointillist
throb of night music
is older, runs deeper
than speech. An electric
flicker the planet's first

incidence of traffic.
Then heartbeat. Then thought.

We sit in the warm dark watching
container-ships ride
on blue-black moonlit glitters.

After long
journeying arrived at the high tide
of silence, after talk.

ACKNOWLEDGMENTS

Poems from this collection have appeared in the following books and magazines, some of them as earlier versions:

Sky News (Rare Object 88, Vagabond Press, 2013) 'At Lerici', 'Entreaty', 'Rondeau', 'A Parting Word', 'Shadow Play', 'Sky News', 'Persimmons: Campagnatico', 'Seven Faces of the Die', 'Ghost Town', 'Australia Day at Pennyroyal', 'Night Poem'.

The Monthly (December 2010) 'A Touch of the Sun'.

Poems 1959–89 (UQP, 1992) 'At Laterina', 'Haystacks'.

The Best Australian Poems 2013 (Black Inc., 2013) 'At Lerici', 'Earth Hour'.

My thanks also to the Scottish Arts Council for the Muriel Spark International Fellowship 2008, and a month-long residence in Edinburgh and at Stromness, Orkney.